Violin Playing and Violin Adjustment

By

James Winram

Published by Forgotten Books 2012

Originally Published 1908

PIBN 1000065317

Violin Playing and Violin Adjustment

.

BY

JAMES WINRAM

William Blackwood & Sons
Edinburgh and London
1908

PREFACE.

IF what I have written should prove to be a help to those especially who are not in a position to obtain the best tuition, I shall be quite satisfied.

It may be stated that this is not a tutor, dealing as it does with the more advanced points of violin playing in the clearest and most concise manner at my command. A knowledge of the rudiments is therefore essential.

The illustrations are from photographs taken specially by myself, in order to make clearer the various positions of the hands and fingers described in the text.

J. W.

2 WARRENDER PARK CRESCENT,
EDINBURGH, 1908.

CONTENTS.

VIOLIN PLAYING.

Contents.

VIOLIN ADJUSTMENT.

ILLUSTRATIONS.

ix

Illustrations.

VIOLIN PLAYING

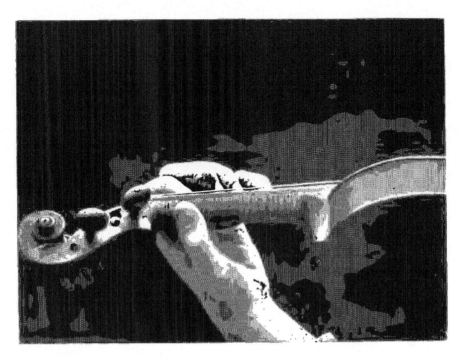

THE NEW WAY OF HOLDING THE VIOLIN.

The tip of thumb is below the level of finger-board.

REGARDING THE NEW WAY OF HOLDING THE VIOLIN.

IN proceeding to give directions as to the holding of the violin, I purposely refrain from introducing any points dealing with what is known as the new way of holding, as after a thorough trial —where of course great care was taken to see that the pupil's practical progress was not interfered with—I have come to the conclusion that at the beginning of a pupil's studies the new way is not conducive to the best results. There is great danger of bad intonation, and this statement applies even to a student whose ear is nearly perfect. The reason is not far to seek, for the left hand—which is weak at the first lessons without being handicapped in any other way—seems totally unable

3

to put the fingers down with either strength or control, until the thumb is projecting above the finger-board a *little*—but mark carefully, only a little. An improvement as regards strength of fingering and surety of intonation immediately follows. As a matter of fact, however, I am not condemning the new way; on the contrary, I entirely approve of it, but *not at the beginning of a pupil's studies.* It should be adopted by all advanced students, and a great improvement in the command of technique will be the result; but the instructions in the chapter on "How to hold the Violin" must be adhered to, and it is only later on that any alteration of the thumb's position should be attempted, as then no harm can result.

THE THUMB PROJECTING CONSIDERABLY ABOVE THE FINGER-BOARD,
AND CALLED BY THE MODERN SCHOOL THE OLD WAY.

HOW TO HOLD THE VIOLIN.

THE reason that so many violin students do not make the progress anticipated is due to the fact that they are in many instances studying with very little conception of how to hold either violin or bow. It is wellnigh impossible to achieve any measure of success under such conditions, and it is to be hoped that the student will be convinced at the outset that too much stress cannot be laid on the injunction here given—viz., to devote the greatest care and thought to the holding of the violin and bow.

The correct way to hold the violin is to place the centre of the chin on the tail-piece ; slant the head over to the left, and the jaw will adjust itself. Bring the instrument well under the jaw, and close

5

Violin Playing.

to the neck. Hold the violin so that it is leaning downwards to the right-hand side. If the violin is held flat, the right arm would require to be raised too high to allow the fourth string to be played on comfortably, and if it is held at too great an angle downwards, the tone on the first string will be weakened.

The position of the left hand should be as follows. Place the thumb about one inch from the nut; it ought not to project too much above the finger-board, and should be pointing slightly out-wards, not leaning over towards the other fingers. The first finger should be placed well back to the nut, so that the third joint of this finger[1] is resting on the neck of the violin, ready to play F natural at any time. **Keep the palm of the hand off the neck of the violin.** It is necessary to pay attention to this, or it will greatly interfere with the student's progress later on if such a fault be persisted in. Everything in connection with the holding of the violin or the bow is of the highest importance. If the left thumb be held inwards every tendon in the back of the hand will be

[1] *I.e.*, the third *joint* counting from the finger-tip.

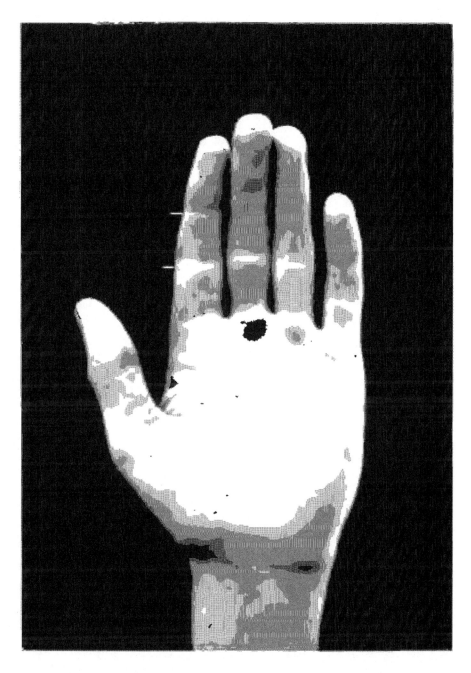

SHOWING WHAT ARE CALLED FIRST, SECOND, AND
THIRD JOINTS.

THE CORRECT BEND OF LEFT THUMB.

THE WRONG POSITION OF LEFT THUMB, SHOWING INWARD BEND.

How to hold the violin.

tightened. Flexibility in the back of the hand, and also in the wrist, must be acquired. In taking a firm hold of anything the thumb comes towards the other fingers (inwards) quite naturally, but if the thumb is bent outwards, the power to grip is considerably lessened. **The arm should be brought well under the violin.** This is very important, so that the subsequent fingering will not be interfered with.[1] This position sometimes causes a slight pain in the upper portion of the arm, but practice and perseverance soon remove the discomfort. The carelessness of the habit observed in many players of resting the left arm against the body cannot be too strongly condemned, and in most cases is the result of laziness.

There has been a great deal of discussion as to whether chin-rests and pads should be used, some teachers maintaining that such aids are unwise. The question can be considered from a common-sense point of view. What is convenient for one

[1] If this injunction be disregarded the motion of the hand when it is ascending into the higher positions will be checked by the body of the instrument. It is necessary that the hand should work between the first and highest positions on a perfectly straight line.

7

Violin Playing.

player in the way of chin-rests and pads will not suit another, but it is nonsense to lay down any hard and fast rule. A simple experiment will prove whether a pad and chin-rest are necessary or not: stand up perfectly erect, and place the violin under the jaw **without lowering the head.** If there is a space between the collar-bone and the back of the violin it must be filled up with a pad. A player with a short neck will probably not need either a chin-rest or a pad, whereas a player with a very long neck will require both.

A pad is simply a small cushion stuffed firmly with cotton wool, and is generally covered with black velvet. If the violinist be a lady, it is better to attach the pad to the violin with the aid of a ribbon. If a man requires a pad it had better be carried loose, so that it can be slipped under the vest before playing. Another little invention for a man is to have a piece of cloth stitched to the inside of the lapel of the coat, so that it can be folded over when playing, and turned back when not required; for the coat lapel gets very much glazed if a great deal of playing is being done. One of the greatest technicians of to-day uses a

THE VIOLIN HELD AS IT SHOULD BE—WITHOUT SUPPORT OF LEFT HAND.

How to hold the violin.

very big pad which enables him to adjust the violin and hold it in position without the assistance of the left hand. *This is how the violin should be held.* The wrong way is to hold the violin *up with the hand.* The pad must be properly adjusted before beginning to play.

If the violin be of value the use of a chin-rest is advisable, as the varnish is worn off the breast to the left of the tail-piece in the majority of old violins, and it saves the instrument from further wear and tear. It also prevents perspiration from sinking into the wood where there is no varnish to prevent absorption. The best kind of chin-rest, therefore, is one that grips round the edges of the violin and at the same time covers the bare part of the breast. There are plenty of these chin-rests to be got. There is no doubt this kind is the best. It acts as a safeguard to the violin and receives the pressure of the jaw, thereby preventing part of the tone from being suffocated.

HOW TO HOLD THE BOW.

THE correct way to hold the bow is as follows. Place the **tip** of the thumb half on the stick and half on the nut of the bow; bend the thumb inwards towards the other fingers, as this is what gives the power to produce tone. The thumb knuckle will now be pointing outwards. The first finger should be in such a position that the stick lies between the first[1] and second joints of the finger. The second and third fingers should be opposite the thumb, the second finger being more directly opposite the thumb than the third. The tip of the little finger should rest on the stick without projecting too far over, unless this finger is abnormally long. By having the stick against

---

[1] *I.e.*, first joint counting from the finger-tip.

10

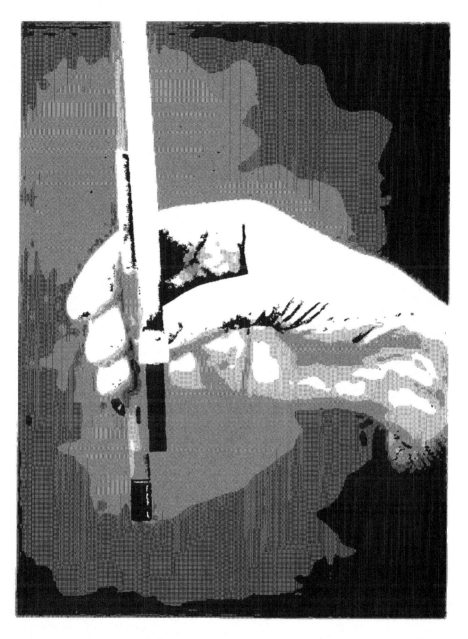

THE CORRECT WAY TO HOLD THE BOW.

*The thumb is pointing inwards to the other fingers, which conse-
quently makes the thumb knuckle point upwards. This is
most important.*

How to hold the bow.

the finger so that it is pressing between the first and second joints, and resting the end of the little finger on the stick, the bow will have the proper slant across the hand, and consequently go parallel with the bridge and finger-board if the arm is working properly. The other fingers should be placed without spreading or compressing them. They will adjust themselves if the thumb, first finger, and little finger are placed as described. There must be no circling of the fingers round the stick ; they should be slightly curved.

If a careful watch be kept on a player whose tone is weak, it will invariably be noticed that *the thumb is not bent inwards*, the chances being that it will be bent outwards. It is useless trying to get power of tone without an inward bend of the thumb.[1] It is very difficult for the beginner to acquire the correct position for the thumb, as the two thumbs are in sympathy with each other, and when the left thumb is pointing outwards the right thumb has a tendency to do the same —viz, to curl outwards ; but this is an error

[1] When the extreme point of the bow is in position on the strings the bend of the thumb is not so pronounced.

which must be rectified if tone be sought. For
when the bow thumb is bent inwards as directed,
the left thumb has a tendency to turn over the
finger-board. Therefore these directions must be
adhered to so as to get independent action of
the thumbs.

There is another point about holding the bow
which must be carefully observed. The first finger
must not curl round the stick, and the latter must
not press on the *third joint* of the finger. This
is one of the most common and serious faults in
holding the bow. The student should try this
experiment, as it would be as well to make the
point clear. The first finger should be placed so
that the stick rests between the **second and third
joints**; at the same time curl the finger round.
Hundreds of players do this, and it is useless
to attempt any of the fancy bowings with the
finger in this position, as the tendon is tightened,
which makes the wrist stiff, further progress being
quite out of the question. By placing the stick on
the finger so that it presses between the *first and
second joints*, any bowing becomes possible, as this
method of holding the bow does not tighten the wrist.

ELEVATIONS OF THE RIGHT ARM.

THERE are four elevations of the right arm, one for each string. When playing on the first string the arm should be close to the body, but not actually touching it. The elevation for the second string is a little higher than for the first string, but the arm should be raised higher still when playing on the third and fourth strings. Put up the violin and draw a down bow on the fourth string till the bow is in playing position at the point. The arm should be lowered slightly to pass to the third string elevation, but there is a difference when passing to the second string, for the arm lowers considerably in its course to that string, showing that the elevations for the third and fourth strings are near each other, whereas

13

Violin Playing.

between the second and third strings the difference is considerable, the elevations for the second and first strings resembling the third and fourth in being in such close proximity to each other.

The upper portion of the arm is used for two purposes—the principal being to cross from one string to another, the arm being worked up and down according to the string the player wishes to reach.[1] The second duty is to begin and complete whole bows. If the bow is not parallel with the bridge and finger-board, the tone will not be satisfactory. Attention must therefore be directed to the working of the down bow, and great care taken to watch that the upper portion of the right arm never comes past the line of the back.[2] If this be not guarded against the ultimate result will be a most shocking style, coupled with a very bad tone. This is what is called "sawing,"

[1] In fast work, however, and where only a small portion of the bow is used, the wrist works the crossing from one string to another, only, however, on adjacent strings.

[2] To render the explanation clearer, suppose a stick were tied across the back, projecting, say, twelve inches or so on either side of the player, then the arm when it came in line with the back would not be able to get farther on account of the stick.

14

Elevations of the right arm.

and must not take place. The down bow should be played thus : place the bow near the nut on the string, and let the bow descend until the upper portion of the arm comes into line with the back. When the arm reaches this position the elbow-joint comes into play ; the forearm should descend, and the full bow is completed with a slight inturning of the wrist. Playing a full up bow, however, is much more difficult than down bow, although the danger of "sawing" is not so great. The point of the bow should be placed on the string ; the wrist moves first, and the upper portion of the arm should meanwhile be practically steady. After the wrist has moved, the forearm should rise towards the strings, using the elbow-joint only, and when it is up as far as it will go, the upper portion of the arm should complete the whole bow, the wrist, the forearm, and upper portion of the arm moving in sequence.

When playing on the first and second strings the bow is worked on the elevation which has been already explained, but achieving the mastery of playing up bow on the third and fourth strings is more tedious. Anything of the nature of down-

Violin Playing.

ward pressure in violin playing is bad, and if the arm is kept on the same elevation all the way while playing an up bow on the third and fourth strings, the tone will be very unsatisfactory. The attention of the student is drawn to the following explanation. When about half of the up bow on the third and fourth strings has been played, the elbow should sink slightly during the latter half. If the bow has been raised all the way while playing full up bows on these strings, the pressure will be downward ; and it is a "draw" across the strings that is required, not perpendicular pressure. Some players curve the wrist too much when playing up bow. It must be distinctly understood that there should be no exaggerated curve on the wrist, for it is useless. An easy curve is all that is required. Subjoined here is a recapitulation of the important points.

Do not draw the arm past the line of the back.

All short bows are played entirely from the elbow-joint and the wrist.

The upper portion of the arm is used for crossing from one string to another, and also to begin and complete full bows.

THE SLOW BOW.

THERE is a mistaken idea among many that a great player when practising a Concerto, for instance, plays it repeatedly from beginning to end. This is not the case. A first-class performer —to keep his playing up to "form" after he has acquired proficiency and gone through the mill— practises exercises that have a great bearing on successful violin playing, and knowing exactly as he does what his principal weaknesses are, gives them the closest attention accordingly. It may be a surprise to some to learn that all the eminent virtuosi have devoted great care and study to one phase of violin playing in particular, the slow bow —that is to say, practising drawing the bow as slow as possible across a string without stopping the action of the bow for a single instant, at the same time producing a tone of good *timbre.*

It seems to be absolutely impossible, however, to convince many violin students that the practising of this bowing is of the highest importance, and should be most rigorously studied. It is certainly monotonous work drawing the bow slowly on one note, but the value of this exercise is inestimable. The reason that so many violinists have practically no " sing " in their playing, is due to the fact that they do not give sufficient attention to the point herein described, and are at the same time inclined to treat the matter with a certain amount of levity, so far as convincing them of its value is concerned. It would be as well, therefore, if those who study the violin accept of the statement that it is the writer's most firm conviction that the slow bow is of all the phases of violin playing *first in importance,* and must be conscientiously studied and treated with great seriousness, thereby conducing to an improvement in the playing that will be more than astonishing in its ultimate result.

To explain clearly what is meant by slow, the

The slow bow.

bow should take sixty seconds to go from one
end to the other: this will necessitate the bow
going very slow, and at first trial it seems impossible. It is done daily, however, and the best
way to time the bow's speed is to put a watch
with second hands on the music-stand, and practise
accordingly. After the bow has started on its
journey, it will be noticed that it stops at every
alternate inch or so, and curiosity is aroused as to
why this should be. It is the pulse which causes
the mischief, coupled with inability on the part of
the student. Practice will overcome the defect and
ultimately produce good results.

After some success is gained in the playing of
this bowing, it will be noted that as the bow gets
within six or seven inches of the point—down bow
—the tone gets weaker. This can be remedied
by exercising more pressure at this part of the
bow. The same fault takes place when playing up
bow, and more weight should be brought to bear
accordingly. But it is the successful playing of an
up bow that is the bugbear of all violinists, for the
principal defect occurs not at the point, nor in the

middle, but when playing with the remaining six or seven inches near the nut. The tone produced there is in many instances of a most unsatisfactory character, and practice is the only cure for the deficiency.

PASSING FROM A LOW STRING
TO A HIGHER STRING.

PASSING from the first string to the fourth string and at the same time refraining from sounding the intervening strings is difficult. Practice should be developed along the following lines. Play nearly a full bow and stop; then pass to the fourth string with that part of the bow which remains without making the slightest sound, at the same time retaining the pressure on the bow. The same principle holds good for the up bow. This should be practised slowly until some measure of success be attained, then gradually increase the speed. The same principle is applied to passing from second to fourth string, and fourth to second; only, of course, fourth to first and first to fourth passes are the most difficult, there being more space to traverse.

STEADINESS OF THE LEFT HAND.

ONE of the most serious faults in violin playing is to slant the hand back from the
wrist to finger notes near the nut. If the habit
be acquired of moving the hand backwards and
forwards, using the wrist as a pivot while fingering, it will be the means of hindering the progress
of the student to a very great extent. Teachers
do not need to look to see that this movement
of the hand is taking place, as there is an un-
evenness in the passage being played which clearly
indicates that this fault is present. It is therefore
imperative *that the hand be kept perfectly steady
while fingering.* In addition, the left hand should
be in such a position that the fingers are in line
with the strings, so that the hand is not turned

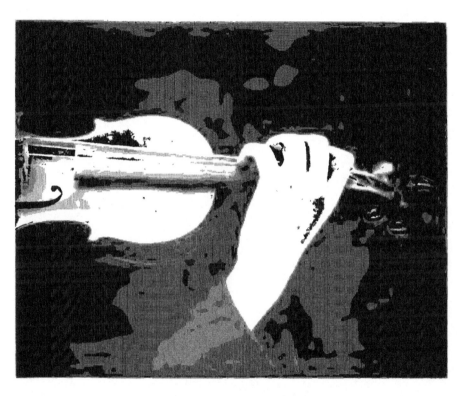

SHOWING THE FINGERS PLACED CORRECTLY IN LINE
WITH THE STRINGS.

THE FINGERS POINTING OUTWARDS.

Showing the hand at right angles to the finger-board—a very bad fault. The fingers should be in line with the strings.

Steadiness of the left hand.

out at right angles to the finger-board. The fault of putting the fingers down in such a way that they fall in at the first joint[1] is a common one, and the consequences will be disastrous if it be not promptly checked, and care taken to see that they go down on the finger-board, having the shape, as near as it can be described on paper, of three parts of a square. The majority of teachers have a very trying time getting the third and fourth fingers of a pupil's hand to go down on the string with the proper formation; and the difficulty is supplemented by an additional trick which the fourth finger has of sinking underneath the neck of the violin when the third finger is put down. This fault is quite readily cured if the proper treatment be adopted, for it is due to the fact that when the third finger is put down on the finger-board and the fourth finger is level with it, the little finger loses its power to stay in its position and sinks,—the third finger having during this period in all probability fallen in at the first joint. If the fourth finger, however, be held higher when the third finger goes down, the

[1] *I.e.*, counting from the finger-tip.

23

fault will be promptly cured, as this finger only displays this weakness when it is on a **level** with the third finger.

It is these little details that cause so much heart-breaking among violin students who are working seriously, and who find that a great many months' practice has been thrown away. Progress is quite out of the question with the fingers working on a wrong method. It is not at the beginning of the studies that these and other faults prove such a hindrance to advancement, but it is only a question of time till further progress is practically impossible. To select one instance as to how this can come about : the position of the finger with the joint fallen in can be considered with regard to what the ultimate result will be when a passage in double stopping occurs. The finger in this instance must be clear of every string other than the one it is stopping, except where perfect fifths [1] occur ; and if the joint of the finger falls in, double stopping cannot be a success, and is near being an impossibility. The injunction already given as regards the steadiness of the hand is important so

[1] See chapter on Double Stopping.

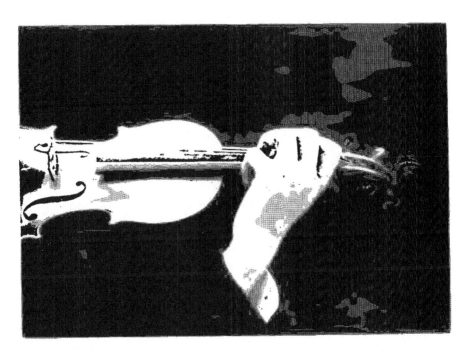

FOURTH FINGER UNDER THE LEVEL OF FINGER-BOARD.

A very bad fault.

Steadiness of the left hand.

far as ordinary fingering is concerned ; but it also applies with added force to the fingering of chromatic scales, which depend so much on absolute steadiness of the hand for their success, and if played other than on this method, the result will be a scale of a whining character. All fingering should be done from the fingers, and the back of the hand should be practically inert.

THE JERK.

JERKING is one of the commonest faults in violin playing. It is most apparent in melodic work at the change from the down bow to the up bow, and *vice-versa*. It produces a very bad effect, and sounds as if the player had been suddenly startled. Many violinists have a jerk in their playing, and are unconscious of having such a fault; indeed in some instances the suggestion that it is present is not very gracefully received. The cure for this, the most general fault in violin playing, is plenty of practice of long bows, taking time at the change from one bow to another, and in observing that the motion of the hand when ascending is continuous with its motion when descending, there being absolutely no pause between.

26

The jerk.

It is imperative that this be done without stopping the action of the bow for a single instant; and it is here that the difficulty arises, which can only be overcome by assiduous practice and an infinity of patience. It is most important that the last three inches of the bow at either end be taken full advantage of in melodic playing. These oft-neglected inches should receive the most rigorous attention when practising to avoid the jerk, and the greatest expenditure of care on their use when drawing a full bow up or down will be amply repaid in the quality of sustained tone.

SLURRING.

SLURRING is the art of playing two or more notes in one bow, and retaining the proper *timbre* in the tone. The chief point to watch in slurring is to move the bow at a pace that will include all the notes in one bow, and at the same time give an equal part of the bow to each note, as it would certainly sound very uneven to give, say, the first four notes of a run of eight notes three-quarters of a bow, and play the other four with the remainder of the bow. The method which should be adopted in practising slurring, is to begin by playing two notes in a bow, then four, and so on, till a great number can be introduced, at the same time giving the same bow value to each note. The phrase may be marked crescendo, but

28

Slurring.

this does not mean that the loudest part of the passage receives the greatest share of the bow. The same rule applies here as before. Draw the bow at the same pace, and give the loudest part of the phrase the most pressure. It is in melodic work especially that faulty slurring is heard. The bow must not stop for the slightest instant while the notes are being played—that is to say, there must not be the slightest halting of the bow. It should be kept continuously moving, and follow on, as it were. This is the whole secret of proper slurring. If a long run of notes in one bow occurs in a piece, the student will perhaps appreciate the advice offered in the chapter on the "Slow Bow," as a long slurred run depends on the bow being equally dealt out for its success. Slurring plays a most important part in phrasing, and when slurred couples occur in the music the bow should be lifted off the strings after each couple, as the not unusual way of keeping the bow on the string is most unsatisfactory. If the music is of a slow nature, the bow should be lifted off quietly after couples. If the music is brilliant, the bow should be lifted off smartly, to put dash and life into the composition.

THE CLOSE SHAKE.

THE number of violinists who use the close shake on a wrong method is legion. Many players, both amateur and professional, completely spoil their playing by introducing a close shake which is cultivated on wrong lines. If such a close shake be carefully watched it will be noticed that it can only go at one speed, and is produced by shaking the forearm and hand very quickly. Coming as it does from contraction of the muscles of the forearm, it is not capable of being regulated to go at any speed. In fact, it were better that no such close shake should be used. The plain notes are much to be preferred.

The following points should be carefully studied. The close shake should be capable of being regu-

The close shake.

lated to go at any speed to add improvement to the tone and suit itself to the various nuances in the music. Anything in the nature of muscular contraction must be rigorously excluded : it should be practised on the following method. Place the left hand in the third position, as it is easier to learn the close shake in this position than in any other. That part of the hand which unites to the wrist should be placed against the lower edge of the violin. It is very essential that this point be carefully attended to, for if the hand is away from the violin, muscular contraction will in all probability take place.

It may be as well to state here that there seems to be a mistaken opinion that the close shake is a flattening and a sharpening of a note. This is not the case. It is a flattening and a naturalising again of a note. After the hand is in position as described, the second finger should be placed on an A natural, third string, third position ; and the whole hand should be slanted or rolled from the A natural to a flatter A. But the student will be surprised to discover that the hand will not move backwards freely. The most important point has now to be described—viz., that the whole secret of a successful close shake lies in the taking of the first finger clean away from the neck of the violin. If this finger is pressing against the violin neck, it surely stands to reason that the hand cannot be slanted or rolled from the wrist : this is the point where hundreds go wrong in practising the close shake, and it is useless to expect progress to be made if the first finger is jammed as described. Freedom for this finger enables the hand to be rolled backwards, and as the instructions up to this point have concerned the backward movement of the hand, it remains to be added that the roll is completed by bringing the hand forward till the finger is again on A natural.

The roll should be practised slowly until the hand moves backwards and forwards in an easy style without either breaks or jerks. It should be, as near as can be described on paper, like the figure 8, one continuous roll. It would not be advisable to introduce it into performance at this early stage, as it is not yet perfect, being much too slow in its movements. It is all there, however, with the exception of two points : these are, that the roll be increased in speed, and the hand should

The close shake.

have less swing backwards and forwards. This will materially assist in concentrating the tone to a smaller point, and make it more pleasant to hear.

It was stated at the beginning of this chapter that the close shake should be capable of regulation so far as speed is concerned, and it would be as well to explain clearly what is meant. In *pianissimo* passages in melodic work, or where tenderness in the tone is needed, the close shake, if worked on correct lines, will assist the performer to gain this effect, as owing to the fact that it is possible to regulate the speed, the hand can be moved slowly, and the swing be almost imperceptible ; the sound will not be increased, but the beauty of tone will be greatly enhanced, factors which will materially aid the performer to render the music with the required sentiment. When music is marked F, FF, or is perhaps of an appassionata character, the close shake rolls faster, and with a wider sweep of the hand, which enables the performer to put dramatic intensity into the composition.

After proficiency has been more or less acquired when the hand is in the third position, an attempt should be made to use the close shake in the first position. It is considerably more difficult to do in this position, but the principle is the same, so far as taking the first finger off the neck of the violin is concerned, but the palm of the hand must be clear of the neck. The violin should be held as stated in the first chapter of this book, thereby making the close shake possible in the first position; as although the violin is supported slightly with the thumb and the finger which is being used, the weight of the instrument does not rest upon these fingers. There should be no close shake in exercises or scales, other than melodic exercises, and it should be judiciously used at all times, as it is quite possible to have too much of a good thing. Beethoven's music will sound lovely with very little close shake, or if preferred with none at all; whereas Wagner's will gain rather than lose by its introduction. The character of the music must be taken into consideration, and good taste will surely be a sufficient guide. There are many who contend that the close shake should never be used, but when we consider that the world's greatest violinists all use it more or less, it surely must have some virtue.

TONE.

———

IT will be admitted by every music-lover that for sheer beauty of tone the violin as an instrument is pre-eminent. The glorious tones produced by some of the eminent violinists of to-day fascinate even the most unmusical. Without, however, casting any reflections on technique, tone may be said to be the main factor in all music. It is therefore the duty of a violinist to give every attention to the acquiring of a fine tone, and to let this be the highest aim in the course of his studies. It is impossible, however, to produce a fine tone without an instrument of good quality, and a correct method of holding the violin and bow.

There is a mistaken opinion prevailing that to

35

Violin Playing.

get a good tone on the violin the fingers must be held down with a very great pressure,—so much so, that the finger-tips get covered with hard skin, and where the fingers are tender actual cuts appear. If a careful examination be made of the position of the strings and the distance they are from the finger-board in the first position, it will be observed they are not very far off; and except, be it noted, in certain phases of violin playing, this theory of exercising severe pressure *at all times* is a wrong one. When the hand ascends into the higher positions, the strings are farther off the finger-board, the natural consequence being that the fingers must go down firmer and the muscles of the forearm must be more or less contracted according to the music, to give the required strength to the fingering. But there is a difference between putting the fingers down properly and firmly and pressing them as if the player were trying to make holes in the finger-board. Many have the idea that if the points of the fingers get very hard this shows that they put their fingers down perfectly; but one person's fingers will get "corny" whereas another's will be quite unaffected.

Tone.

It depends entirely upon the nature of the skin. The fingers, as has already been shown, play an important part in the production of good tone; but the main elements are the right hand and forearm.

There are two points one must aim for in tone, power and quality. A strong arm is therefore necessary to produce a full tone, as there is not the slightest doubt but that players with strong arms have the greatest tones. A student with a weak arm is very much handicapped; and this much is certain, that if the tone be small there will be a want of "click" about the fingering as well. Deficiency of muscle can be remedied. A systematic course with light dumb-bells will be an aid to better results so far as power is concerned. Practising with the dumb-bells for a week and then discontinuing the exercises is only so much labour in vain. They should be continued. Ysaye and Kreisler are very strong men, and when playing a Concerto finish the solo with the same power and beauty of tone as they displayed at the beginning,—an effect only to be attained by their strength being sufficient to allow reservation. Some teachers are to blame for their pupils producing puny tones, as they persist in telling the pupil to keep the wrist loose. Now, although a loose wrist is a necessary part of a "violinist's outfit," it does not need to be quite in this condition while playing a melody. Though there must be no stiffness, something more serviceable than looseness of wrist can be introduced for melodic work, and that is the power to contract the muscles of the forearm at will and regulate this contraction for the various shades of expression.

It is surprising the number of players there are who play with the bow near the finger-board. It is useless for any one to try to extract a big tone with the bow in this position, as the tone is very weak there. It is only a fine line which separates a big tone from a very rough one; and it is owing to these two kinds of tone being in such close proximity to each other that so many players produce weak tones, for when practising with the bow near the bridge it may slip past this "boundary line," the result being a shocking noise. The bow is at once brought away from the bridge nearer the finger-board, where the tone is for the time

Tone.

being more pleasant, but very weak. Needless to say, this line cannot be seen, but practice will give the feeling when this very dangerous line has been reached. It is acknowledged that the finer the instrument the nearer the bow can approach to the bridge without causing any unpleasant sound.

Having dealt at some length with power of tone, quality of tone now demands consideration. Power of tone depends largely on physique for its production, but quality is the outcome of skill. Ysaye, of all the great violinists, in my opinion produces the finest quality, and sometimes plays in the softer passages with a tone of a very mysterious character. It certainly has a most charming effect, and may be called a veiled tone. It was stated at the beginning of this chapter that the violin is pre-eminent, but the 'cello is more fascinating when this tone is produced by some of the eminent 'cello virtuosi who are in possession of instruments by Strad. or other famous makers. It is practically impossible to write directions as to how this tone can be acquired, as the whole matter would require to be explained verbally to ensure a certain measure of success. The following hints, however, may be of service. The bow should be held as loosely as possible,—so much so, that if any one should "rub" against the player, the slight concussion would be the means of knocking the bow out of the hand. The left hand also plays an important part in the production of this tone, as if the fingers are put down too severely the mysterious quality will be completely eradicated, and contraction of the muscles must be conspicuous by its absence. There is one other point which must be attended to. The weight of the bow must be kept off the strings, and though a slight huskiness in the tone will likely be heard when practising, perseverance will remove this defect. It may be as well to state that a slight undercurrent is not audible when the player is on the concert platform. The whole subject of tone can be summed up in a couple of sentences. The louder the passage, the more the muscles are contracted. The quieter the passage, the more relaxed are the muscles. All nuances can be produced from these two standpoints.

SHIFTING.

THE correct method of shifting is in a great many cases entirely misunderstood. What is meant by shifting is going from one position to another, and it is astonishing the number of players there are whose shifting is on wrong lines from the beginning of their solo to the end. All shifting that *is not slurred* must be played as cleanly as possible—*i.e.*, no sliding of the fingers between the notes, a fault which produces whining sounds. But where notes are slurred, the shifting is worked on a totally different system. Take for instance the following:—

Violin Playing.

The note B is in the first position, and the note G is in the third. There are scores of players who shift this on a wrong method, as they slide with the fourth finger to reach G, instead of sliding[1] so far with the first finger. There are two rules, and if adhered to, shifting is quite easily understood. They are as follows:—

Always lead with the finger in use, never the finger that is going to be used. *This refers to slurred shifting.*

When shifting from one position to another, and the notes are not slurred, they should be played quite cleanly, without any sounds between the notes.

These rules are too condensed in their information to be quite understood by the student, and it would be as well to explain them more fully. Taking, again, the example already given, namely, B to G, it should be practised on the following lines:—

The first finger should lead, that is to say, slide slightly along the string until the third position is reached. The cunning of the hand soon enables the

[1] The word "lead" is used in preference to sliding, as there should be as little of the latter as possible.

Shifting.

student to feel when this point has been reached. When the hand stops, the first finger being on the string would sound the note D, in the third position; but this is exactly what must not take place. The first finger should lead until the hand is nearly at the third position, and then the fourth finger must slip in as it were, and go down on G, just as the hand stops travelling, consequently preventing the D from sounding, although the first finger is still on the string, and by this time also in the third position. All slurred shifting is worked on this method, for whether it is in going from a low position to a higher one, or coming from a high position to a lower one, the principle is the same,—lead with the finger in use. It does not matter whether the leads are long or short. Personal intuition soon enables the performer to know when the hand has gone far enough, and all leading must be done with good taste, no unnecessary whining between the notes.

There are other points to be dealt with and very important.

Always go from an open string to a note in any position cleanly, whether *slurred* or in *separate bows*. To give an example, play A open string then D first

Violin Playing.

finger second string, third position. Any attempt at sliding the first finger from the first position must be promptly stopped, as this is the most shocking fault in shifting. There may be some scepticism about the matter by some, but they can easily prove it by asking some cultured singer to sing the two notes here given, A and D. They will sing these two notes cleanly, without any sound between the notes ; and if ever a violinist does anything on the violin that would be considered bad in vocalism, the sooner it is stopped the better. It is surprising that some teachers should maintain that the finger in going from an open string to a note in the positions (slurred), should slide along the string, and start from nothing as it were—*i.e.*, from inside the peg-box behind the nut. This contention is too absurd ever to receive the slightest consideration.

The next point to be dealt with is what is called single finger-slides—that is, going from second finger to second, third finger to third, and so on. They are quite easily managed so long as the performer fingers with the necessary amount of slide in keeping with good taste, for it is very easy to overdo it. The slide must be in keeping with the character of the

Shifting.

music. There are quite a number of very telling effects to be got by a process of fingering which is much in use at the present time, and is an imitation of the inflexions of the voice. The following illustration will show what is meant—

and the passage should first be played with the fingering marked above ; but if the same passage is played with the fingering subjoined below, it will be admitted that vocally it is a great improvement.

There is a tendency to use the latter style of fingering too much, and while a little of it is very refreshing it becomes very tiresome if introduced too frequently.

THE INFLUENCE OF THE POSITION OF THE LEFT THUMB ON TECHNIQUE.

THE position of the left thumb is quite plainly portrayed in the illustrations, both as regards the new way and what may be called the old.

It has already been stated that the new position of the thumb is not recommended for beginners, but when the student is sufficiently advanced the change of the thumb's position produces astonishing results. It will be noticed that the tip of the thumb is below the level of the finger-board, and it is due to this that the advantage is gained, as the thumb can dart quicker and cleaner to the higher positions, whereas the other position for

Influence of position of left thumb.

the thumb tends to retard the rapid movement of the hand. If the two positions are considered, not from any scientific aspect but from a common-sense point of view, it will be seen that the whole matter resembles a race between two athletes of equal calibre, but it would be a very unfair race, as the one having a start from the other makes it a foregone conclusion which would win. It is the same with the two thumbs; for it surely stands to reason that the one which is nearest the socketed part of the violin neck must get there first, and hence produce more satisfactory results. The new position for the thumb, although called new, cannot be described as such, as a great many professionals play this way without ever knowing they are doing so, and why? They were not taught to do this; but when they become sufficiently advanced to use the close shake, where the first finger must be off the violin neck, feel that their thumb would need to be of gigantic proportions to keep it in the old position, at the same time taking the first finger off the instrument. Being able to do the close shake better and more comfortably with the thumb below the

47

Violin Playing.

level of the finger - board is a minor detail in comparison with the important influence the thumb has on technique, and before a player can hope to get three-octave scales, long runs, &c., to work sweetly and without breaks or "kicks" in their centre, the muscles of the thumb must be very highly developed. This is where the great weakness occurs in hundreds of violinists, and if carefully watched it will be noticed that they cannot play a three-octave scale without making an effort to get the hand against the violin for support in coming from the top of the finger - board to the first position. This is due to the muscles of the thumb not being sufficiently developed to enable it to move independently while playing the scale both up and down, the consequence being that the passage is unequal, and it will never be perfect until the hand goes up to the top of the finger-board and comes back to the first position on a perfectly straight line, without the slightest deviation of the hand to one side or the other. Technique can only be a success if worked on these lines.

DOUBLE STOPPING.

DOUBLE stopping is the art of playing two notes at one time, in tune, and with a nice quality of tone. It is difficult, but if played with method can be made much easier. There are many who, when playing double stopping, put the fingers down at random with the inevitable result. Others who try double stopping make no headway, owing to a deficiency of musical ear. It very often happens that a student, though having a perfect ear, can make no progress whatever, hears that the notes are out of tune, gets very angry and disgusted with the whole business, and feels inclined never to touch a violin again. But in many instances the difficulty of getting correct intonation in double stopping is caused not so much by the inability of

49   D

Violin Playing.

the player who has a perfect ear, but because the strings are not likely to be in exact register to each other. An explanation is necessary.

It is practically an impossibility for any one to play double stopping on the violin unless the strings are in exact register to each other, so far as thickness is concerned. If one finger is put down properly, on the square, **covering two strings and two notes** at one and the same time, and the bow is drawn across the two strings, the interval played is a perfect fifth. If this fifth be out of tune the strings are not in register, and double stopping is out of the question. It is simply heart-breaking the way a great many students string their violins. Thick second strings, thin thirds, the others wrong, and all out of relation to each other. No progress can be made under such conditions.

No teacher can instruct in double stopping, but he can give hints that will prove useful. It is, however, a question of *a perfect ear*, and practice. The general opinion is that there are two kinds of ears,—the musically perfect ear and the other which is musically void. Nothing was ever wider of the mark. The variations which occur are aston-

Double stopping.

ishing, and without discussing them individually we may select one kind of ear which specially concerns us here. There are many violinists who undoubtedly play single notes in tune, but play very much out of tune in passages with double stopping. They cannot separate the notes in their ear, and although practice eventually creates a marked improvement, the defect always more or less remains.

The next important point the student must devote his attention to is to acquire a fine tone while playing double stopping. *If pressure is applied* to keep the bow on both strings at once instead of *balancing* the bow, the tone will be very rough. This is a very common fault, and it bears a striking resemblance to the slow bow, so far as the importance of practising drawing the bow slowly on two strings is concerned—watching that the bow never leaves one or other of the strings for a single instant. It is very difficult, however, to convince students of the importance of practising these details, which contribute so much to the making of a violinist. It is only by having the fingerboard and the notes thereon imprinted on the mind that double stopping can be a success. The fingers must go down at *the same time*, and the student should know the exact relationship the notes bear to each other, so far as distance from each other is concerned. Stoutish fingers are best for violin playing, though the general idea is that long pointed fingers are the most suitable. As a matter of fact, the latter kind handicap a player.

VARIOUS BOWINGS.

THERE are one or two bowings which every student must practise thoroughly to be able to do justice to the passages where these bowings occur. A splendid exercise, and one which can be utilised for many phases of violin study, is the second exercise in " Kreutzer." It is a well-known one, and its appearance is very deceptive, for on first sight it looks remarkably easy, but on the contrary it is very difficult to play well. It may be taken for granted that no other known exercise is so useful for the practice of bowings, and before any attempt is made to use it in this way, a thorough knowledge of its notes must be acquired, so that it can be played from memory. The notes should be played first slowly, with full bows, taking care

Violin Playing.

to observe that the notes are all natural, for the continual introducing of F natural on the first string and B natural on the second string will lead to bad intonation, owing to these notes not being opposite each other, if the student is not on the alert. It will be as well to turn back to the chapter on "Steadiness of the Left Hand," wherein it is stated that the hand must never slant back from the wrist to finger notes at the nut. The hand must remain absolutely steady while playing the Kreutzer exercise quoted above, and it is here that the first finger must do its work correctly. The best way to get the first finger to play the notes without any slanting back of the hand is to practise without the violin,—first of all, by locking the finger, as it were, until the point is touching the top of the palm. This is how F natural should be played at all times, and it is astonishing how clean a passage sounds when the hand is kept absolutely steady. In fact, any other way of fingering means failure.

Attention should now be directed to the various bowings, and the first example is of great service in getting the elbow-joint to work correctly, for

FIRST FINGER LOCKED FOR PLAYING NOTES
NEAR THE NUT.

*All notes near the nut should be played with the first finger
locked, as the not unusual way of slanting the hand from
the wrist is one of the most serious faults in violin playing.*

Various bowings.

"sawing" is more often in evidence during a passage with this bowing than at any other time.

It will be noticed that the notes are bowed as follows : two slurred and two separate. This bowing should be continued to the end of the exercise. Play the two slurred notes with a full bow, and the two separate ones at the point ; then a full bow for the next two slurred notes, and the two separate ones near the nut. This should be practised slowly until the elbow is working correctly, then increase the speed. The same bowing should be practised, but only using half the bow, first the upper half and then the lower half, adopting the same principle as when a full bow is used.

The same notes should be used for the various bowings, as the notes can be altered in form to suit. The following is a most valuable exercise and a great improvement on the not unusual way of playing it down and up bow. It is called the reversed bowing, and is played by beginning with an up bow first, and if properly done is the very

Violin Playing.

acme of neatness. The whole secret of getting this bowing to work properly is to bring the bow back to the point with a smart jerk of the wrist each time the short note is played. If this is not attended to, the bow will gradually work its way down till the other end of the bow is reached —viz., the nut end. The notes take the following formation :—

and the same notes can be used for this other example, which is called two in a bow :—

It will be noticed that there is a dot on every second note, which means that the bow must be stopped absolutely dead between each two notes, but of course taking care to observe that the notes are not equal in length. This exercise should be practised first with full bows and then with half bows, till a thorough mastery of it is acquired, as this bowing is very much used.

THE SPRINGING BOW.

THERE is certainly a great deal of charm about this beautiful bowing, and there are not many who do it perfectly. Some of the great players fail to do it justice, but their other great qualities carry them to the front in the profession. The following instructions should be carefully read. Lay the bow on the strings and put a finger on any note. See that the bow is on the string where the bow is balanced. No exact spot can be defined as to where this is likely to be, but it will in all probability be about the middle, and can be found with a little experimenting. Every bow has its own balancing point, and after this has been ascertained the bowing should be tried, but without the slightest attempt to put spring into it. That will come later.

Violin Playing.

What is wanted first of all is to get the correct action of the wrist. The bow should be held as loosely as possible, so that the wrist will be flexible. Move the bow slowly and use the wrist alone, making little strokes, taking care to notice that these strokes work with a side movement of the wrist both in up and down bow. There must be no up and down movement of the wrist. The arm must be kept quite steady. After this has been practised, make the bowing go faster, and it will now be impossible to keep the arm perfectly steady, as it must certainly participate in the bowing, but only to a slight extent, the movement being at the elbow-joint. The faster the bowing goes the more the elbow moves, and if the wrist is loose and working sideways, that spring which has been so much coveted will come into the playing if conscientious practice be done. It is certainly worth all the trouble expended on it.

The instructions up to this point have concerned the sideways movement of the wrist, but a more difficult branch of springing bowing has yet to be acquired, to keep the bow springing while working alternately on two adjacent strings. This is diffi-

The springing bow.

cult, and requires a great deal of practice. The movement in this case is totally different from the sideways movement of the wrist, and is acquired by moving the hand *upwards* and *downwards* from the wrist, crossing from one string to the next adjacent string with the smallest possible movement.

It is quite unnecessary to use the upper portion of the arm here to cross from one string to the other. The wrist will manage it beautifully if worked on the following method. Place the bow on A, open string, and pass to E, open string, by lowering the hand from the wrist, and when passing back to A open, raise the hand from the wrist. On looking at the curve of the bridge and laying a straight-edge on top of it, or on the illustration in the chapter on "The Bridge," it will be seen that the first string is not so very far off the level of the second string, provided, of course, the arm is on the proper elevation. The wrist will certainly do all that is required in the way of crossing from one string to another when the notes are played alternately on two adjacent strings, and where short notes with springing bowing are required.

CHORD PLAYING AND ROSIN.

IT sometimes happens that even the great players fail to keep roughness out of the tone when playing a series of big chords with down bows. Ysaye in my opinion is the finest living player, as his tone is the *beau idéal* of beauty, and he never " scrapes," even when tackling a series of big smashing chords. The whole secret of acquiring a fine tone when playing chords is to allow the bow to descend a certain distance *before* it touches the strings, or, to make what is meant clearer, the bow *should be in action before it strikes the string*, and then *float over the other strings*. The two top notes of a chord should be the most dwelt on, so as to give breadth and dignity to the music.

It is essential to see that the bow is not loaded

Chord playing and rosin.

with rosin. Why so many players persist in putting so much rosin on the bow is more than I can
understand, as the finest quality of tone is produced
when very little rosin is used. If the bow has an
excess of rosin there will be great danger of harsh-
ness in the tone, and chords especially will sound
very rough, although there must be sufficient rosin
to prevent the bow slipping.

While writing on the subject of rosin it remains
to be added that cheap penny packets of rosin are
useless, and responsible for a great deal of "screech-
ing." Rosin in its natural state is not in a fit condition for violinists to use, as it requires to be
neutralised with fat or some other substance to
take the "bite" out of it, and before rosin can be
freed from impurities and made suitable for high
class work, it must go through a process of refining
in addition to neutralising. This undoubtedly shows
that first-class rosin must cost a fair price, and it
is out of the question to expect to buy it for a
penny a packet.

Slight friction is what is required to make rosin
go on the bow as a powder, as it melts at a very
low temperature, and an excess of pressure when

Violin Playing.

rosining will raise heat, thereby putting glazed sur-
faces on the hair and on the rosin. This state of
affairs makes matters very uncomfortable for the
violinist. Half a dozen rubs from end to end of
the bow is all that is necessary.

ARPEGGIOS.

ARPEGGIOS—or, to give the exact plural, Arpeggi—are very sparkling, and produce a splendid effect when properly done. The bowing is not very difficult to play when simply slurred, but where the notes are marked with dots on top in addition to being slurred, then the difficulty arises so as to get the correct "flutter" on the bowing. The notes may be in groups of threes or fours, but the more strings employed for an arpeggio the more brilliant will be the effect. It is quite possible to play a group of four notes on two adjacent strings, such as the following—

but if these notes are played on four strings as below, the effect will be greatly enhanced—

It is difficult to describe on paper how arpeggio bowing is acquired, but the following points should be noted. The bow is held loosely. The arm should work up and down as a whole, using the wrist at the same time. The weakness in all arpeggios is that the two bottom notes in groups of four—viz., the last of four and the beginning of four—do not receive sufficient attention. The same fault occurs when the two top notes are played—the last of four and the beginning of four.

The best way to practise arpeggios is to play them with ordinary slurring first; every note must be distinctly heard. This is essential, as it is so much labour in vain attempting to "flutter" the bowing until this is acquired. After proficiency in this respect has been to a certain extent attained, the student should try to introduce the "flutter"

Arpeggios.

over the strings.   The best way is to flick the wrist,
and this hint will enable the student to understand
what is required, as the bow must get a start, and
this is the way to start it.   One of the great secrets
of arpeggio bowing is *to turn the bow over slightly
towards the bridge.*

STACCATO.

WHEN the notes are marked with little perpendicular strokes thus, ' ' ' ' ' ', this means that they must be played at the point of the bow with very short bows, and with force. The secret of good staccato playing is to see that the bow is absolutely stopped after each note, or failure will ensue. It is difficult to stop the bow absolutely dead after each note with separate bows, and even more so in a run of staccato notes in one bow, but the patience and perseverance demanded by its study are amply rewarded when a thorough command of this bowing has been attained.

The above illustration is known as " The Staccato,"

Staccato.

and requires a tremendous lot of practice before perfection is attained. It is played with the upper portion of the bow starting from the point, and the notes must be as short and crisp as possible. This staccato must come entirely from the wrist. It is no use whatever trying to push it through with the muscles of the forearm contracted, as it can only be done this way—and a very unsatisfactory way it is—at the one speed which suits the performer. The wrist should be working perfectly, so that the staccato can be regulated to go at various speeds. The point that staccato coming entirely from the wrist has a limit to its speed will be dealt with later.

Down bow staccato is played on exactly the same principle as up bow, the only difference being that in down bow the bow must lean over slightly towards the bridge. It is not surprising that players should become confused about the dots and dashes over notes in music, which both mean staccato. The dashes have already been explained, but it is generally recognised that the presence of dots means that the bow has to be lifted off the string after each note, as this sign is commonly used where the notes have to be played lightly. Confusion is often caused by wrong staccato marking by careless or incompetent editors. In cases of this kind the character of the music should be a sufficient guide.

Advanced players will probably be familiar with passages of this nature :—

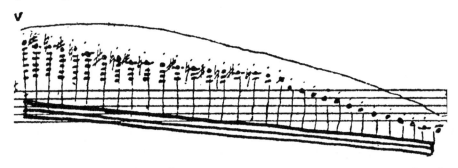

The Wienawski school of composers are very fond of introducing it, and it certainly has a most electrical effect when properly performed. It is called "Flying Staccato." It looks a terrible affair on paper, but appearances are again somewhat deceptive. The half tones lie so close together on the higher reaches of the finger-board, that it would be absolutely impossible for any one to play the above chromatic scale with different fingers, although it is often attempted. There is only one way to do it : practise drawing the fourth finger along the

Staccato.

first string from E harmonic at the top of the finger-
board till the hand comes into the first position. Do
not try to introduce staccato in the meantime. Practise this glide till it works perfectly smoothly and
without the slightest break. As was remarked before, staccato to be neat and capable of regulation
must come entirely from the wrist, but this statement does not apply to " Flying Staccato." This
form of staccato cannot be done from the wrist
alone ; it goes so fast that the wrist, which is
the *main element*, is inadequate, and help must
be called in from certain muscles of the fore-arm.
It is impossible to describe exactly on paper where
these muscles lie, but they are immediately above
the elbow-joint, and this part of the arm only should
be drawn without contracting *any other* muscle of
either arm or wrist. It can be done. Practise the
staccato only on the open string until it has got
the necessary shiver upwards, as the bow must
never on any account come back after going forwards. The student should then try the staccato,
and at the same time draw the fourth finger along
the string from the E harmonic as already explained.
Watch what happens: the semitones are so very

Violin Playing.

close together for a considerable distance that as the finger passes over the notes the bowing picks them out in the most beautiful manner possible. Remember that the finger passes over the string slower near the top of the finger-board than it does near the first position, where the semitones are larger. The hand must therefore travel slightly quicker as it approaches the first position to make the difference in the size of the semitones. All this, however, has only taken the run to B first position, and the passage has yet to be completed. When the first position has been reached then follows the most difficult part to do, as the fingering and the bowing must fit together exactly, or this part of the run will be a failure.

HARMONICS.

THERE are two kinds of harmonics, natural and artificial. The natural harmonics are played by placing one finger on the string. Artificial harmonics are produced by putting two fingers on a string. The most important point about the playing of natural harmonics is *the keeping of the left hand perfectly steady*. It cannot be too strongly impressed on the pupil's attention that if there is the slightest movement of the hand other than the fingers while playing natural harmonics, the rendering of the passage will be a failure. In playing natural harmonics the fingers should go on the string very gently—in fact, should just alight on the string as it were, the bow just having sufficient pressure to make the tone satisfactory.

71

Violin Playing.

As stated before, artificial harmonics are played with two fingers—viz., the first finger and fourth. The first finger, which goes *down* firmly, "stops"

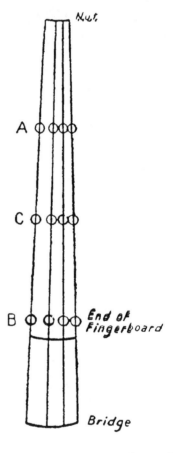

A two octaves above the open string, harmonic (first finger, third position).

C one octave above the open string, solid or harmonic.

B two octaves above the open string, solid or harmonic.

the melody, and the fourth finger goes *on* lightly, thereby producing the tune in harmonics. If the first finger is not stopping the notes in tune, the fourth finger will follow suit and produce harmonics

---

that are also out of tune. Another method of playing artificial harmonics is to put both the first and fourth fingers on the string lightly : this gives the same effect as the firm stopping of the first finger, but the tone is considerably weaker. The illustration on the previous page should be carefully studied.

From the bridge to the letter A is the same distance as from the nut to letter B, thereby giving harmonics of the same pitch two octaves above the open string ; but the notes at C are one octave above the open string, as the string is divided here into two equal parts. Note that at letters B and C the notes, if played solid,—*i.e.*, with the fingers pressed down,—will give the same notes as are got when the fingers go on lightly on the same places, and produce harmonics identical in pitch with the solid notes. The notes, however, at letter A give different notes when played solid and harmonic, having not the slightest relationship to each other.

PIZZICATO—RIGHT AND LEFT HAND.

THE bow should be held firmly with the second, third, and fourth fingers; and the sign " pizz." means that the notes are to be played with the first finger or two fingers of the right hand instead of with the bow. The word "arco" means resume the bowing. The thumb should be placed in such a position that half of the thumb-tip is on the violin and the other half against the finger-board. The best quality of tone is got by placing the thumb about one inch from the end of the finger-board. The student should be careful to pull the strings horizontally, for if they are pulled on the perpendicular the strings will "bizz." Pizzicato chords are played on a different principle, the bow

74

Pizzicato—right and left hand.

being held with the thumb, second, third, and fourth fingers, leaving the first finger free, and which should pull across the strings on the slant.   Left-hand pizzicato is very difficult, and is denoted by crosses above the notes, as follows :—

It requires a great deal of practice to produce it with a full tone, and the whole secret of being able to accomplish this is to swing the hand out at right angles to the strings when taking the fingers off, at the same time putting leverage on the first finger at the nut.

[1] The notes without crosses are played with the point of the bow.

THE MUTE.

THERE is great diversity of opinion as to whether violin solos should at any time be played with the instrument muted. Some of the smaller pieces are very pretty when played *con sordini*, and the greatest players include them in their programmes.

There have been many arguments as to whether a metal or a wooden mute is the better, but it would be advisable to be provided with both kinds, as they have each their merits for various occasions. A metal mute weakens the tone too much when used in a large concert-hall, and a wooden mute gives better results, as the tone is fuller when the latter is used. It is not advisable, however, while playing, say, in a drawing-room, to use a wooden mute, as

The mute.

---

it gives off a nasal quality of tone that is not so pleasant to listen to close at hand ; and on the whole, a metal mute will give better results under such circumstances.

The best mute for orchestral playing is un-doubtedly the spring mute, which is constructed on the same principle as a tie - clip. There is nothing more distressing at an orchestral concert than the sound of stiffly - fitting mutes being snatched off the violins after a soft passage has been beautifully played. The spring mute removes all annoyance to conductor and audience, and its use should be insisted on by those in authority. It sometimes happens that a player forgets to bring a mute, a substitute being provided by fix-ing a coin between the strings behind the bridge. This is a stupid proceeding, and should not be encouraged.

When the mute has only a slight grip on the bridge, the tone is more powerful than it would be were the mute severely pressed down. If the grip is too slight, the vibrations when playing will in all likelihood loosen the mute's hold, until it ultimately rattles with each stroke of the bow.

77

Violin Playing.

This must be avoided, and care should be taken to see that both sides of the mute are gripping the bridge; as if one side only is firm enough, the other side will rise during the solo, thereby causing annoyance to the performer. Muted solos, however, if played too often get very tiresome.

THE STRING QUARTETTE.

THE string quartette is the finest of all chamber music, and when a student is proficient enough he should arrange to become a member of such a combination. The craze of the present day among violinists is to become a great soloist, but to be a fine quartette player—which necessarily means being a good musician—is a higher aim. It is quite an easy matter nowadays to arrange string quartette parties among musical friends, and very pleasant evenings can be spent.

It is a matter for regret that when the very best performers of string quartettes visit certain towns, the public do not lend more support by patronising their concerts, thereby giving the players encouragement in their work. There seems to be

Violin Playing.

only one way out of the difficulty, — we must rely on the musical amateurs, who have advanced greatly within recent years. The cultivation of string quartette playing among amateurs should always be encouraged, although there are opinions to the contrary, as it is only by their aid that first-class performers will be encouraged to continue their chamber concerts and give the ideal renderings of the works which are so educative.

It may be asked, How are we to rely on the amateurs? The question is easily answered, for when string quartettes are more cultivated, as they are being at the present day, the taste for this class of work will be fostered, and larger audiences will be the result.

A very good plan, after the quartette party has been arranged, is for each member to buy a standard quartette, or where a club is joined the music of course is provided out of its funds. There should be a distinct understanding among the players that there must be no *tempo rubato* as in solo playing, or the second violin, viola, and 'cello being too subservient to the first violin. If the members of the quartette are men of common-

The string quartette.

sense, and anxious to make progress with their art, matters should go smoothly, as nothing tends to disorganise a quartette quicker than one of the members who has had experience, and is perhaps fitted to give instructions to the others, doing so in a way that gives offence. It is quite an easy matter to give advice diplomatically.

The custom of playing several quartettes in one night's practice cannot be too severely condemned. One quartette should be studied, and an understanding as regards the nuances is a *sine qua non.* The attack is very important, and should be played without the slightest wavering. All the expression marks must be played with the correct colour, as it is in these subtleties that a quartette fails. Crescendo on PP, for instance, is very often played wrong owing to the increasing loudness being too great, considering the crescendo begins from PP. Singing a member's part who has lost the place in the music, thereby making him feel very uncomfortable, may afford amusement to the others, but this should be promptly stopped, or the chances are he has come to the practices for the last time.

SOLO PLAYING.

EVERY violinist who has to earn his living must get a connection either as a soloist or as a soloist and teacher combined. Sitting at home and depending on the favourable criticism of a few friends never yet made a career for any one and never will. There are many eminent players, however, who abstain from playing in public. The reason is not far to seek. Either they have become lazy, and will not practise, or they are too cunning to go on the platform to damage an already acquired reputation. But these players have proved their worth, and can afford to some extent to rest on their oars.

The worst enemy the concert performer has to contend with is undoubtedly nervousness. This can be overcome to a great extent. A little nerv-

Solo playing.

ousness is a blessing in disguise, for a performer never puts the same amount of dramatic intensity into his work when thoroughly cool as when a little nervous. This is an undisputed fact. Coolness is only an invitation to carelessness, and it is worth while considering what it is that to a great extent at least makes soloists nervous.

There is a well-known maxim in connection with the game of golf which can be applied to the concert performer with added emphasis, " Don't press "; and it is a very valuable one. For if there is one thing more than another that causes unsatisfactory performances on the platform it is pressing, and trying to do too much. The soloist sets out with the firm intention of excelling himself ; and it has been proved to be the case that more pressing, less success.

Consider, for instance, a singer who is anxious to give his very best performance, and forgets that there is a very valuable asset called restraint. What will the result be ? It is invariably the case that the performance is spoiled, owing to the forcing of the tone, which is caused by over-anxiety. The same can be said of solo-violinists, and it would be as well to offer a word or two of advice and encouragement to the student when making his first appearances in public.

The solo is yet to be written that will please every one, for if a slow melody is played it may be described by some as having been too dreary, and a fast sparkling solo is criticised as being too jumpy. Such criticism is at first very discouraging, but the best plan is to work hard, never study any music but what is of the very best, and pay no attention to side remarks that are only meant to wound. It is quite an easy matter to know when one is in the company of a candid and experienced friend who has a knowledge of the subject. Advice in this case is of value, and a criticism from such a source should be accepted and thought over.

The general health must be attended to if the nerves are to be right. For those who can spare the time, a long walk into the country makes a splendid nerve tonic on the day of an important concert. Eating heavy meals just before the concert is only courting failure, and fasting is just as bad. Many violinists who smoke stop this habit on the day of an important concert to steady their nerves, but this is altogether a mistake. The writer had

Solo playing.

the pleasure of being introduced to Ysaye in the side-room of a concert-hall after he had finished playing the Beethoven Concerto, and was surprised to find him smoking a long pipe which held at least one ounce of tobacco. He had to play later on the evening, but he knew exactly what to do to steady his nerves, and appeared to be quite happy and contented with his pipe.

Worrying and fidgeting before the concert causes nervousness, and the whole secret of getting over the discomfort is to remember not to press, and to play with the necessary restraint. But no : the desire, natural enough, is to play above the previous standard, and cause surprise by the excellence of the performance, the consequence being that the solos are played at the highest tension, and not likely to be a success. It may be as well to add that the audience are not slow to see when a performer is straining every nerve, and suffer dis- comfort just as the performer does.

Music is much more enjoyable to listen to when the performer is in reality or apparently at his ease. Solos should in every case be played from memory if at all possible. The student should try to culti-

Violin Playing.

vate good style, and the common habit of swaying while playing should be promptly stopped by all who have tendencies that way, but without going to the other extreme of standing in too stiff an attitude.

The bow should be handled gracefully and without exaggeration of style, such as swooping the bow round in three parts of a circle before playing a down bow. This looks very affected, and does not improve the music. In playing a slow piece the bow should be lifted off at the last note of a slow ending quietly, whereas if the piece ends vigorously the bow should be dashed off briskly.

Some performers depend largely on tricks for a good deal of what is apparent success. Many a first-class performer receives a very poor reception owing to his not being an adept in tactics, and in most cases does not care whether his performance is met with vociferous applause or not, as he is too much concerned as to whether he did justice to the music. If a musical tactician is recalled for his solo, he generally bows his acknowledgments; but it is a well-known fact that the British public, when they see that the performer has apparently decided not to gratify their wishes, at once make up their mind not to be baulked of the encore. Then follows a pleasant sort of passage at arms, which the performer carefully keeps going as long as he can do so with safety. The result is commonly what is described as a tremendous reception: yet the performance may have been a very jerry affair after all. Every performer who has had a few years' experience knows all these tricks. I merely mention these points so that when the violin student makes his first appearances he will not be discouraged if a singer who sings rubbishy songs should carry off the palm of the evening. Singers are the worst offenders in the matter of tactics, for when they see that things are going badly with them at a concert they seldom scruple to change the programme,—put on another piece that is sure to be some catchy song with a good top note. The result is inevitable. But there is always a section of the audience who, being educated musically, smile at all this byplay, and it is to them that the true artist must look for encouragement and support.

ONE OR TWO POINTS TO REMEM-
BER REGARDING CONCERTS.

———————

1. IF there is a fire in the side-room of the concert-hall the player should stand in its vicinity for some time, violin in hand. This will take the cold air out of the violin and prevent the strings from breaking by the sudden transition from a cold case to a heated hall.

2. The violin should not be held with the hand circling round the neck of the instrument, as this heats the strings.

3. The A string of the violin should be *tuned a shade sharper* than the A of the piano. This will bring the D and G strings of the violin in tune with the piano. These remarks apply to a piano that is in perfect tune.

Points to remember regarding concerts.

4. Care should be taken to see that the violin is tuned properly, as it is very essential that this be done.

5. If the piano is too far away from where the violinist is intended to play, the arrangement should be altered at rehearsal. The violinist should stand near the pianist.

6. A heavy violin case and a bundle of music should never be carried by a soloist to a concert-hall, as this makes the hands shaky.

7. The violin and bow should never be laid on a side-room table, or they will be sure to meet with an accident.

VIOLIN ADJUSTMENT

THE HAIR OF THE BOW.

EVERY violinist should thoroughly understand the characteristics of bow hair, as it can be the means of causing serious inconvenience under certain conditions.

Horse-hair in its natural state is studded with numerous spikes which are practically invisible to the naked eye. It is by these projections rubbing on the string that tone is produced. The long fibres on which these spikes rest are useless for violin-playing minus the spikes. If the hair is worn it follows that the spikes are practically all removed. Playing with the stick of the bow will give nearly as good an effect as that produced by worn-out hair. The consensus of opinion seems to be that so long as there are plenty of hairs in

Violin Adjustment.

the bow it does not need re-hairing. It is not a question, however, of the number of hairs there are in the bow, although these should be the right quantity, but in what condition they are.

If a lot of playing is being done the bow should be re-haired at intervals of two to three months, and in exceptional cases once a-month. It sometimes happens that the first string of the violin breaks repeatedly at that part where the bow plays on. This proves conclusively that the bow hair is at fault through being worn done, and new hair will put matters right.

Rosin which clings so tenaciously to new hair should be sparingly used after the first rosining, as the spikes retain a firm hold of the powder for a considerable time. Putting rosin on old worn-out hair is simply useless, as the rosin falls on to the violin when the first few strokes are made with the bow. It is quite a simple matter to have the bow re-haired nowadays. If there is no one who can hair a bow in the player's vicinity it should be sent by parcel post to some one who can do so. Bow boxes for sending bows by post are supplied by the dealers, and can be used repeatedly ; failing

The hair of the bow.

that, the head of the bow should be rolled in cotton wool, and the whole placed between two pieces of wood,—quarter inch thick will be quite strong enough. The parcel should then be wrapped in brown paper, and in most cases will travel quite safely. If the bow is of value it can be insured by paying a small sum at the post office. Compensation can then be claimed in the event of any damage being done in transit.

THE VIOLIN PEGS.

THE pegs are capable of giving a great deal of trouble to a violinist, but it is certainly surprising to find so many players with them in the most wretched condition,—so much so, that when the violin is being tuned the pegs "jump" instead of working smoothly. This is the fault of the person to whom the violin belongs, as it is quite a simple proceeding to put them right. But although the pegs are put into first-class order this does not ensure perfect working, as the greatest care must be taken to see that the strings are running straight into the peg-box. If they are crossing each other, smooth working is impossible.

If the strings will not go straight into the peg-

The violin pegs.

box, this shows that the holes in the pegs are in the wrong position, and new holes should be bored as near the side of the peg-box as possible. It is quite easy to bore new holes with a small borer, which should be inserted crossways to the reed of the wood to prevent splitting. After boring from one side, and the borer is just making its appearance, bore from the other side. It may be as well to explain, before proceeding further with instructions regarding the various adjustments, that the directions which I am submitting are for those who are not adepts at using tools, and whose stock of repairing utensils will in all probability be very limited. I may state without any undue egotism that I know all about the experts' way of working so far as violin repairs are concerned, but the hints given here are not for experts. Take, for instance, the instructions already given regarding the boring of the pegs. It certainly takes some time to bore violin pegs by hand, and it would never pay an expert to waste time ; so he has a small drill running on the turning lathe[1] whereby he can bore holes in a dozen pegs before

[1] Failing which, a hand drill is used.

Violin Adjustment.

an amateur could bore one. There is a very fine instrument for tapering the pegs; it does it quickly and beautifully, working as it does on the same principle as the pencil sharpener, which was much used at one time. To make a slight digression from the pegs, I have refrained from giving any instructions about the finger-board, and its being kept perfectly level, as it should be, as the holes which get worn in it are bad for the player and worse for the tone. But it is absolutely useless any one attempting to level the finger-board without a steel-faced plane, and very few amateurs are possessed of such elaborate tools. Those who have steel-faced planes can easily level the finger-board by first removing the nut. Insert a thin knife between the nut and finger-board, and it will soon come off. To revert to the pegs, however, they should work smoothly, and it is quite an easy matter to adjust them. They should grip at both shoulder and point, and it is readily seen where they are gripping, as the peg will polish at that part if given a few hard turns when in the peg-box. If the polish is only at the point, file till the shoulder comes into position. After both

The violin pegs.

shoulder and point are gripping, rub with No. o glass-paper. They should then work smoothly if the strings are not crossing.

Rosin, chalk, or black lead should not be rubbed on the pegs to make them hold. The best plan to make the pegs work very smoothly is to rub on *a little very hard soap*, and give the pegs one or two turns when in position to work in the soap. The violin should be tuned while the performer is in playing position. It is easily done if the pegs are fitting properly. The left hand only should be used for this purpose, and the not unusual practice of lowering the first string after playing should not be adopted.

THE SOUND-POST.

THE sound-post is the most important adjustable part of the violin, consisting as it does of a small pillar of wood standing inside the violin. It is remarkable that such a tiny piece of pine can, practically speaking, either make or mar the tone. If the violin be without a sound-post the tone is almost *nil*, but the moment this small post is in position the instrument gets new life as it were, and responds to all the demands made upon it consistent with its rank.

There is a craze among amateurs, and even in some professional circles of the present day, to be always tampering with the sound-post, but it were better that the violin be submitted to an expert repairer, who will examine it thoroughly, and who

The sound-post.

should know, by the tone of the instrument and on looking at the sound-post, if it is in its correct position. It is just possible, however, that the following instructions as to the adjustment of the sound-post may be of assistance to those who are anxious to learn the necessary details in connection with its exact setting.

The sound-post, as has already been explained, is a pillar of pine wood with a straight reed running through it. Its place inside the violin is almost immediately behind the foot of the bridge, first string side. There are some experts who maintain that there is an exact spot that the sound-post should always be on, but the opinion is confidently advanced here that there is no rule for that exact spot. There is, however, a half-inch radius that the sound-post must be in, and the slightest deviation from the place which suits the violin will mar the tone.

Every violin has its own position for the sound-post, and the wood that it is made of must be of a nature such as will suit the violin to get the best results. The pine may be soft, medium hard, or hard, and it is very difficult even for the expert to

Violin Adjustment.

be always able to judge which of these woods will suit the violin to be operated on. It requires years of experience to be able to fit a suitable sound-post in position with the master hand. If a violin which is of a hard-wooded nature requires a new sound-post, it would give unsatisfactory results in most instances if the wood of the post were also hard, and if a violin of soft wood were fitted with a post also of a soft nature the tone would not be a success. It has invariably been proved to be the case that hard-wooded violins are the better for a sound-post made of softer wood, but with soft-wooded violins the reverse will give equally good results.

Sound-post setters are included in all dealers' lists, and cost a very small sum. The setter should be used with extreme care, as it is a very easy matter to make dents in the F holes while working with it, and a violin that has badly damaged F holes has lost a good deal of its bloom. A piece of wood should be selected that will be likely to produce good results. It should be rounded until it is, say, a quarter of an inch in thickness. Sometimes a violin is the better for a thin sound-post, but experience only could teach this. The sound-post

The sound-post.

must in every case be able to go through the F hole comfortably, as there must not be the slightest attempt at forcing it through. If it is too tightly fitted the vibrations will have no play, the consequence being that the tone will not carry; if it is fitting too loosely the vibrations will be far too rampant. Tight-fitting sound-posts and loose-fitting sound-posts are both unsatisfactory, but the tight one is the worse of the two, as this is what cracks the violin under the back. (*Vide* chapter on " Violins Old and New.")

A loose-fitting sound-post may stand in its position all right when the strain is on the strings, but it will in all probability fall when the pressure is off. This should be remedied by supplying a longer one. A sound-post which falls when the first string breaks should be immediately discarded. The writer once had a curious experience when playing : a sound-post travelled from behind the bridge along the inside of the violin owing to the vibrations, until the reduced diameter of the violin put a stop to its travels,—the post being then found to be standing perfectly erect.

It cannot be too strongly urged here, that in

Violin Adjustment.

taking out a tight sound-post it should be done without the slightest attempt at forcing, or in all probability the setter or the hand will smash the breast of the violin when the post gives way.[1] The best proceeding in any such circumstance is to lay the violin on a table covered with a soft cloth: a long thin tool should then be introduced at the "F" hole, placed in such a position that the end is pressing near the bottom of the sound-post without touching the back of the violin. A few *slight* taps with a *small* hammer will be all that is necessary to remove the post. When a new post is fitted the old one should be used as a guide for the exact size, and when in position should fit comfortably when the bridge is off the violin, being neither too tight nor too loose.

The ends should be cut with a very sharp knife to fit the shape of the violin, or failing which, file with a very fine file. Cutting is the more preferable method, however, as this leaves the grain of the wood free, whereas filing only hardens the ends and thereby destroys some of the wood's

[1] An expert would insert the setter at the F hole, fourth string side, and pull the post down.

The sound-post.

vibratory character. The setter should be inserted near the middle of the sound-post, in such a position that the post will go into the violin to stand with its reed running crossways to the reed of the violin breast. The following illustration will show exactly what is meant.

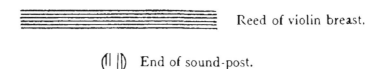 Reed of violin breast.

(⎮⎮ |⎮) End of sound-post.

After the sound-post is inside the violin it should be put behind the foot of the bridge, first string side ; and if the instrument is a high-breasted one the post should be close up to the bridge, but never underneath it. If the violin is flat-breasted, the post should be away from the bridge a sixteenth to a quarter of an inch or more accordingly, so as to get the best results.

If the fourth string is weak in tone the post should be brought nearer the **first** string side, whereas if the first string is weak move the post nearer the **fourth** string side, and a satisfactory setting will be accomplished, using these two points as a guide. Great care should be taken to see

Violin Adjustment.

that the post is *never moved with the full strain on the strings*, as this makes holes in the violin breast inside. The ends of the sound-post must fit exactly, and although the end which is resting on the back of the violin can be seen quite plainly, it is only by inserting a piece of mirror glass, say three inches long by one inch broad, at the F hole, that the end which is against the breast can be examined while the violin is strung ; but when the strings, bridge, and tail-piece are off the violin, the ends of the sound-post can be examined by looking through the tail-button hole. They are quite readily seen if the instrument is held up to a good light.

THE BRIDGE.

THE bridge as an adjustable part of the violin is next in importance to the sound-post. Every player who has had the misfortune to break the bridge on his violin discovers in most instances that when a new bridge is fitted the tone is not so good as it was before the accident happened, and the violin is not likely to recover its former characteristics until the new bridge and violin have been in conjunction for some time. A violin of little value may be fitted with a new bridge every week without causing much variation of the tone, but when an old bridge gets broken, which has been part and parcel of the violin as it were, the difference of tone when a new one is fitted is very marked. This is not imaginary,—it is too true.

Violin Adjustment.

Bridges as sold in the music-shops are not in a fit condition to go on a violin without first being prepared and fitted : and when a new one is required there should not be the slightest hesitation in purchasing the best that can be procured. It is therefore quite unreasonable to expect that a first-class bridge can be bought for twopence [1] which will give satisfactory results fitted on a good violin. Some experience is necessary to be able to judge what density of wood will suit the instrument best, and the grain of the wood should be carefully examined. Some are wide in the grain and others are close. These grain lines are quite visible, and are of importance in the selection of a bridge. If sparkle in the tone is desired, a hard-wooded bridge—*i.e.*, a close-grain [2] one—should be chosen, whereas if a softer tone is preferred, it can generally be got with certain other conditions by fitting a bridge with a wider grain.

[1] A great many bridges are sold at this price, but they are not satisfactory.

[2] There are exceptions, however, to this theory, but they rarely occur, as the grain lines are harder than the wood which is between them, the consequence being the more grain lines the more difficult to cut.

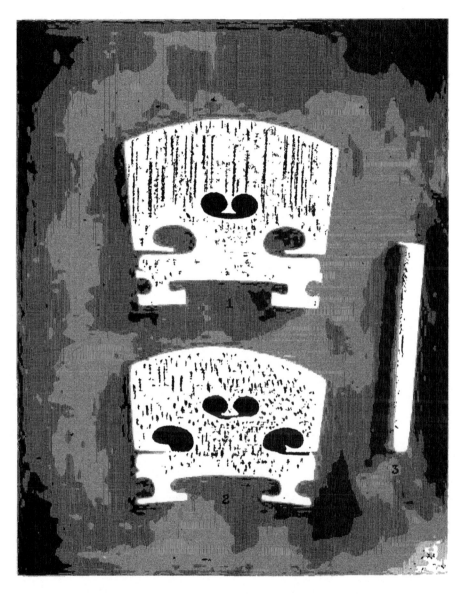

1. THE BRIDGE AS IT IS WHEN BOUGHT OUT OF THE MUSIC-SELLER'S.
2. THE BRIDGE PREPARED READY TO GO ON THE VIOLIN.
3. SOUND-POST SHOWING MARK WHERE SETTER IS INSERTED.

The bridge.

The first proceeding in the preparing of a bridge is to see if it is too thick, as this has a very important bearing on the tone. The thickness should not be more than three-sixteenths of an inch at the bottom and tapering to one-sixteenth at the top; for if there is too much wood the tone will be muffled. A very good way to reduce the thickness all over[1] is to lay the bridge flat on a piece of glass-paper not too rough in texture and rub carefully, as the feet are very fragile and liable to get broken.

Attention should now be directed to the feet, which require great care in fitting, so that they lie on the breast of the violin perfectly. A very sharp knife should be used for this purpose, working the blade sideways and also on the perpendicular. The bridge should be marked on one side with a pencil, so that it will always be put up in the same position when fitting, as the breast of the violin is sometimes undulating at that part where the bridge stands, and the feet in such a case would require to be cut with different formations to fit exactly, as they

[1] An expert would use a steel-faced plane, and plane the bridge to the correct thickness.

Violin Adjustment.

must do at all times, without the most infinitesimal space being seen between the breast of the violin and the feet of the bridge.

The bridge should then be cut the exact height. Opinions differ as to what the height should be when the strings are in position. In most cases the strings should be a quarter of an inch off the finger-board at the bridge-end, but no hard and fast rule can be laid down, as if the player is very muscular a higher setting should be cut accordingly, and if the fitting is for a young lady whose fingers are probably not so strong, the bridge will be cut lower.

An important piece of work has now to be undertaken — viz., to cut the bridge with the exact curve on top, as some are flat and others are nearly round. Both are bad, and the proper curve should be studied by the illustration so as to give clearance when playing, and at the same time not cause defects in the working of the right arm : these will occur if the bridge is not cut on the correct form, for when the curve is too pronounced the fourth string side will be too low, the consequence being that the arm would require to be raised higher than it should

The bridge.

to allow the fourth string being played on comfortably and without apparent effort. The first string side is cut lower down than the fourth, as it should be.

After the bridge is rounded and nicely finished off with No. o glass-paper, the incisions[1] for the strings should be marked off; and a knife should never on any account be used for this, as the strings should lie on the bridge, not sinking into holes. A small round file should mark very slightly the place for each string, for if the strings are down into the bridge the vibrations will be partly chocked. In marking these places care should be taken to see that they are not put equally apart. The incisions in the illustration will show exactly how they should be. The first and second strings lie more close together than the second and third, which are farther apart, and the third and fourth are wider still, as the fourth string requires more room for vibration than the others. As to the exact distances between the incisions other than the relation they bear to each other, no rule can be laid down.

[1] The incisions in the illustration of bridge are shown deeper than they should be for learners.

Violin Adjustment.

A man with thick fingers would require the strings to be farther apart to suit him, whereas the strings should be brought closer together to suit a lady with a small hand.

When the violin is being tuned, care should be taken to see that the bridge is not falling forward, as this is what causes the majority of accidents to bridges, and if slanting forward should be put right at once, so that it will be standing erect, and if anything leaning over slightly towards the tail-piece. If this be not observed the bridge may fall, and the chances are that it will get broken. In addition, the falling of the bridge may split the breast of the violin.

There is a very bad system at the present day among students of cramming a bulky lot of music into the violin - case on the top of the instrument. If this habit be persisted in, the possibility is that some day the neck will part company with the violin. The bridge should be wiped with a soft cloth, as silk is apt to catch and take a corner off; also, be it noted that no liquid should be used for cleaning the bridge, as it is bare wood.

STRINGS.

IT seems to be absolutely impossible to purchase a
violin first string for solo-playing which can be
relied on not to break, and also in addition will not
be false, whistle, or " miss fire." The reason a string
is false is because it is not the same thickness all
the way along. The writer has long come to the
conclusion that after considerable experience Italian
strings are by far the best. These strings fray, but a
string which does this is to be preferred to a string
that breaks without warning. A string that frays
will stand a lot of wear and tear before a player is
forced to take it off. Students when they see a
string of this class fraying think it is going to break,
and put on a new one, but a fraying string will hold

Violin Adjustment.

on to the bitter end. A cheap few-strand string is of a different nature, for when one of the strands breaks the others are not able to bear the strain, and the inevitable result follows. A string should be pure gut, spun, and matured without *artificial heat*. This class of string if spun with care will give the best results, as its vibrations are free. The Italian strings are made on this principle, and are the favourite strings of a great many violinists. There is a good deal of luck in buying a bundle of violin strings, as one bundle may be very good, whereas the next lot may be more or less false.

Strings are made from the entrails of lambs or sheep, but the lambs provide the best string. If a bundle of Italian strings are bought and break one after the other, they are too new. This can be remedied by laying the others aside for a month or two to mature, which will make the fibre firmer and thus give the string a longer life. Various theories have been put forward to test a string for falseness, but there is only one, unfortunately, and that is to put the string on the violin and play on it. Part of a false string can often be saved by cutting, say,

Strings.

four inches or so off the end, and if still unsatisfactory, other two inches can be removed, till a
length equal in thickness is got, but such a string
is never satisfactory, seeing that part of it has been
round the peg.

VIOLINS OLD AND NEW.

I T is very difficult for amateurs, and even for
professionals, to judge a violin properly unless
they have had a great deal of experience, and are
frequently handling violins of different nationalities.
It is impossible to give more than a bare summary
of the subject in a chapter of this book. The writer
has especially studied the subject of violins, and in
addition has experimented with violin varnishes.
The first essential of a violin, to enable it to have
the right tone, **is the varnish.** This statement will
doubtless meet with a great deal of adverse criticism,
but the theories advanced here have been deliber-
ately formed after a considerable experience, and
may be carefully studied by those interested.

If the student is in want of a violin, and has five

Violins old and new.

to ten pounds to spare, a new violin is recommended, as an old violin which can be bought for this amount is generally not of much account. There are plenty modern violin makers who make a fairly good instrument for such a sum. It is advisable to buy from a man who is modest about his abilities, as the best work is often done by those who say least about it. In every case, however, where it can be afforded, an old violin should be purchased. There is such a great deal of trickery, however, in the selling of old violins, that a few hints are given here so that the student can be on his guard against being deceived.

The first consideration when buying a violin is to see that there is plenty of wood in it. This can only be judged by experience ; and the customary habit of placing the thumbs under the F holes, the other fingers on the back, and pressing the violin, should never be attempted by a novice, as it is a very easy matter to crack the violin inside without the crack showing on the varnish. An expert may be seen feeling a violin all over, and the uninitiated may think he is sqeeezing it ; but this is not so. If a violin is cracked inside, the breast must come off before it can be repaired.

Violin Adjustment.

It is quite an easy matter nowadays to get an experienced friend to examine a violin and find out if there is enough wood in it, for a violin that has too little wood is useless. If the violin is a high-breasted one, there should be more wood, so as to get greater resistance in the tone, but the flat model is best.

The inside of the violin should be carefully examined for lining. A great many old violins have had their edges built up. This is easily noticed, as there is a fine hair-line running round the centre of the edges; but lining here does no harm. It is lining inside which is the blemish. Numerous old violins have had the wood thinned by misguided repairers. When modern repairers get such violins to restore, and see how deficient they are in this respect, they line them here and there with very thin layers of wood to give resistance to the tone. But the device is almost always a failure, on account of the glue which binds the two woods together. The advice offered here is not to buy violins which have been much lined. The natural question to ask is, How do you know if the violin is lined? It is quite a

Violins old and new.

simple matter to find out. Slacken the strings, and take off the tail-piece and bridge till the tail-button can be pulled out. Hold the violin up to a good light and look through the tail-button hole. If there is lining present it is quite readily seen; but it is necessary to examine the violin for some time until the eyes have become accustomed to the semi-darkness inside.

Always insist on having a violin costing a good price home on a week's approval, unless an expert examines it. The student is advised here to keep cool, or he will regret it. The usual proceeding is to collect the whole household into the drawing-room to hear the wonderful instrument; but the chances are that in a week or so it may not be sounding quite so well, and one or two weak-nesses and faults will have begun to assert them-selves. The violin on approval has been described perhaps as Italian, but has it got that lovely soft creamy varnish peculiar to Italian violins? If not, it is not likely to be Italian, and if it be Italian without the original varnish the price goes down, as the modern varnish on it will have destroyed nearly all the Italian qualities of the tone. Ex-

Violin Adjustment.

amine the scroll carefully, as if the varnish on the scroll is not the same to the very letter as that on the violin, it is not the original one; at least, it would be better to decide on its merits from this point of view. If a violin is not in one complete whole by the same maker, the value depreciates considerably.

The back of the violin should be carefully examined to see if it is cracked underneath the sound-post. This is a very bad fault. A cross fracture of the breast is a most serious fault, and needless to say a violin with this flaw is correspondingly less valuable.

Many violins have been and are being made that would give as good a tone as the old masters if they had the one thing lacking, the varnish. No violin, however well made, and no matter how old the wood may be, will ever compare with the old Italian violins until the varnishing is done on the Italian method. Italian violins are the finest in the world. There is a mysterious something about their tone that no other violins possess, and I repeat it is all a question of the varnish. If a violin is varnished with a spirit varnish, the tone

Violins old and new.

will be hard. On the other hand, if the varnish is of a too elastic nature, the tone will fog. The right tone will only be got on modern violins when the varnishing is done on the right method. That method is, in my opinion, to be discovered yet. It is not intended to convey the idea that any cheap violin varnished on the old Italian method would equal a Strad. in tone. The violins would require to be the very best that are being made at present. The violin makers of to-day have a far greater selection of wood to choose from than the old masters had, and some splendid pieces of pine can be got from old buildings that are being pulled down. But is there any virtue in very old wood for violin making? I do not think so. On the contrary, I would prefer wood cut from the tree and carefully seasoned for six or seven years for making a violin, to wood over two hundred years old, which is so much coveted by some violin makers. There is quite a brisk trade done at the present time in wood for violin making, and in these days of railways, telegraphs, &c., the modern violin makers are equipped up to the hilt with the finest woods in the world,

Violin Adjustment.

which are cut, seasoned, and sent to this and other countries for their special benefit. It is proved beyond dispute that the old Italian makers had small choice of wood. They were continually patching, but they could patch. Vuillaume, the famous French maker, could make a violin as well finished as Strad. If he had been possessed of Strad.'s varnish, and had used wood that was always "unfaked," he would have surprised the world. As it is, the tone of a Vuillaume is not to be compared with Strad., but given the varnish and unfaked wood, "Strads." would have had to come down in price, or Vuillaumes would have gone up,—the latter most probably.

There are some splendid varnishes on the market at the present day; but can the makers put it on? Varnish that can be peeled off, thereby exposing the bare wood, is not the proper coating for a violin. The point where in my opinion makers of the present day go wrong is that they cannot make the substratum right. This should be part and parcel of the violin itself, thereby coating the violin with a substance which

Violins old and new.

seals the cells neither too tightly nor too loosely. Therein lies the whole secret of the Cremona tone,—*of this I am most firmly convinced.* Violin varnish of the present day lies on the violin too independently, and when we get the substratum right the tone will be close, crisp, and pearly. The violin makers of the present day turn out some really glorious work, and while the tone is good,—and in some cases very good,—to me it is not the right tone. It will come yet, however; but different methods will have to be adopted with regard to the varnishing.

This is not a climate for varnishing violins. A first-class maker would be well advised to have a dozen violins in the white, take the first train for Italy and varnish them there. Climatic influence has an incalculable effect upon the varnishing of violins. How can the violin makers of this country expect violin varnish to dry when it is quoted in Messrs Hill & Son's magnificent book on Stradivarius that he (Strad.) is sorry for the delay owing to the non-drying of the varnish? Varnishing violins and hanging them in a green-

123

Violin Adjustment.

house to dry is futile. Varnish needs atmosphere to dry it. Once the mysterious substratum is discovered,—as it ultimately will be,—the first-class violins of the present day will be every bit as good as the Cremonese, and the price of Strads. will come tumbling down by leaps and bounds. The secret of Cremonese varnishing, when it is discovered, will most probably prove to be a simple one. The contention of some makers that amber is the basis of Cremona varnish is in my opinion without foundation of fact. Those who can dissolve amber seem to think that to know how it is done is a secret. If any one is convinced that amber is the basis of Cremona varnish and wishes to dissolve it, all that he has to do is to buy a bulb of very fine glass from an optician. This will stand a great heat. The amber should be broken into little pieces and dropped down the neck of the bulb, and a little linseed-oil added. The whole should be held with a pair of tongs over a fire at a white heat, and when there is a cloud of vapour ascending the chimney from the bulb the amber is dissolving. After it is cool thin with turpentine. There is a great deal of furniture in Italy at the present time covered with the old Cremona varnish, so far as its quality and texture are concerned, although of course the all-important colours are lacking, as the secret of the latter was possessed solely by the violin makers. The substance of the varnish, however, is on the furniture, showing that it was in everyday use, and as common as turpentine in this country. It is ridiculous to imagine that violins and furniture were varnished with such an expensive gum as amber. It would be interesting to know what amber really is after it is dissolved. Is it still amber? If it is, how is it that turpentine takes no effect whatever on amber in the raw, but will remove amber varnish off the violin?

All kinds of gums have been experimented with for violin varnish; but there is no doubt that Strad. knew nothing of foreign gums, and when the highly complex question of the origin of his colours is considered, it is probable that the constituents were ready to hand in his own vicinity. Perhaps flower heads or roots were the main elements; but it

Violin Adjustment.

should be noted that amber under very simple processes changes its colour completely, thereby proving that the colour of gums can be altered before dissolving, and the necessity for the introduction of foreign substances to provide colour may be some day discovered to be absolutely unnecessary.

Printed in Great Britain
by Amazon